TREVOR

PRACTICE BOOK
for the
flute

BOOK 4
Intonation
& Vibrato

44N08-268050

Order No. **NOV**120550

NOVELLO PUBLISHING LIMITED
14-15 Berners Street, London W1T 3LJ

For WILLIAM BENNETT – In Admiration

CONTENTS

A PREFACE TO BE READ

TO THE STUDENT

This book is about practising; how to extract the most from it, how to be more efficient at it and how to isolate and overcome some of the difficulties of the flute. It is by no means intended to be definitive. It was written to help you achieve good results with many of the flute problems, in the shortest time.

If the exercises are practised properly, it will shorten the time spent on the building blocks of flute playing, and so allow more time for music making.

These points about practising in general, are important:

(a) Practise the flute only because you *want* to; if you don't want to – don't! It is almost useless to spend your allocated practice time wishing that you weren't practising.

(b) Having *decided* to practise, make it difficult. Like a pest inspector, examine every corner of your tone and technique for flaws and practise to remove them. Only by this method will you improve quickly. After glancing through this book, you will see that many of the exercises are simply a way of looking at the same problem from different angles. You will not find it difficult to invent new ways.

(c) Try always to practise what you *can't* play. Don't indulge in too much self-flattery by playing through what you can already do well.

(d) As many of the exercises are taxing, be sure your posture and hand positions are correct. It is important to consult a good teacher on these points (see page 9 in Practice Book VI—ADVANCED PRACTICE).

GUARANTEE

Possession of this book is no guarantee that you will improve on the flute; there is no magic in the printed paper. But, if you have the desire to play well and put in some reasonable practice, you cannot fail to improve. It is simply a question of *time, patience* and *intelligent work*. The book is designed to avoid unnecessary practice. It is concentrated stuff. *Provided* that you follow the instructions carefully, you should make more than twice the improvement in half the time! *That is the guarantee.*

TO THE TEACHER

This is one of a series of basic exercise books for players of all ages who have been learning from about a year up to and including students at music colleges and universities. There are some recommended speeds, but these should be chosen to accommodate the ability of the player. Some exercises are more difficult than others: take what you feel your students need.

TREVOR WYE 1982

FOREWORD

This Practice Book is concerned with everything which affects or relates to playing in tune.★ It may, in places, confuse you. Don't worry. In time, all will be clear.
Reading through this book will not give you the instant ability to play in tune. Play the exercises in each section carefully and often. The acquisition of an 'ear' does not come easily, and, when once obtained, needs constant refreshment.
Without practice, the ability to hear very small changes in pitch and to discern faults in intervals can soon be lost. The ear becomes 'blunt' if not put to work often, as any piano tuner will confirm. To get the most out of this book you will need a few basic tools: a tuning fork, access to a well-tuned piano, some basic adjusting tools for your flute, but, most important of all, time, patience and intelligent work!

The growth in small electronic tuning machines has made easy the whole process of learning to play in tune and checking your instrument.

If it isn't possible to buy one, then borrow one for a few days. What it can tell you, especially about the third octave, may be surprising.

★The exercises for achieving this can be found in VOL.I - TONE pp.34-6 and in PROPER FLUTE PLAYING pp.20-1.

THE CHORD OF NATURE

For this first experiment you will need a piano which is well in tune. It is not important, at this stage, if the piano is totally above or below pitch though it *must* be in tune with itself. First, open the lid wide. If it is an upright piano remove the top front. The fasteners for this can be found just inside the top lid on the left and right. Find a bass note on the piano which is rich, vibrant and in tune — some notes have two or three strings each — it is important that the note has no sourness. Play the note forte and see if you can hear more than one note sounding softly above your chosen note. With practice, you will soon hear eight or ten different notes sounding together above your chosen bass note. To help you hear these notes more easily, play the bass note (in the example, it is F) with one hand, with the other strike the octave above, briefly:

You should hear the octave sounding together with the bass note. The short note doesn't *make* the upper note sound; it simply draws your attention to the note you should listen for.

Now continue with the exercise below. Allow about ten seconds for each held bass note as some of the upper notes become apparent only after a few seconds have elapsed.

Do not use the pedal.

By now you will have heard most, if not all, of the upper notes. These are called *harmonics* or *overtones* and have a definite relationship to the bass note or *fundamental*. If you have some difficulty in hearing any of these notes, move the position of your head a little.

Now for another experiment; after listening to all the harmonics, hold down the sustaining pedal, and sound your low note again. You will clearly hear all the harmonics sounding as a rich chord, rather like an organ:

For the next experiment, without holding down the sustaining pedal, you must push down the key for each of the short notes, or harmonics, in turn *without the hammer hitting the string and causing the note to sound,* and strike your bass note again loudly. After about one second, release the bass note. Listen.

Repeat for all eight notes separately. Taking the damper off the upper note allows it to sound in sympathy with the harmonics of the bass note. This is called Sympathetic Vibration. Some sympathetic notes sound rather louder than others.

To experience more sympathetic vibration, hold down the sustaining pedal and sing a note loudly into the piano.

Now try different vowel sounds: *Oooh, Aaah, Eeeh etc. Notice that the piano 'plays back' the original sound. This is because each vowel sound has a different mixture of harmonics.* REMEMBER THAT THE HARMONICS *NEVER CHANGE THEIR SEQUENCE:* what makes the sounds alter is the relative strength of each of the harmonics in the vowel sound. The understanding of this fact is important to any study of tone or intonation because the fundamental tone of all musical instruments is exactly alike; the reason why we hear differences between say, a flute and an oboe is primarily because the flute has few harmonics sounding with any note (about five) and an oboe has many (about thirteen)⋆. Why do we hear a difference between two different flute players? Because the sound each player makes − though playing the *same* notes with the *same* harmonics − contains different *quantities* of each harmonic. If flour is the basic ingredient of a cake, then varying the quantity of fruit, eggs, sugar and butter will produce different cakes, though the ingredients remain the same.

Try the piano experiment with a different piano and you will have less difficulty in hearing some harmonics and more difficulty in hearing others, especially the seventh harmonic. Piano makers deliberately try to suppress the seventh harmonic because it sounds so out of tune with the natural note on the piano:

Once again play your bass note:

Fix your ear, after a few seconds, on to the seventh harmonic. Now softly play the minor seventh on the piano:

There is a slight but discernible difference in intonation. Which is right? They both are! The natural note has been tuned (or adjusted) to conform with Equal Temperament without which it would be impossible to play in all keys. More of this later in the section headed SCALES.

⋆The starting transient is the scientific term to describe the first fraction of a second of a note and is the other determining factor which helps us recognise different musical sounds.

Here is a list of the Harmonic Series up to the eighth harmonic. There are, of course, many more beyond the first eight, but this list will serve us for now.

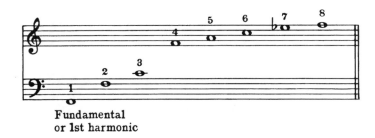

**Fundamental
or 1st harmonic**

Another harmonic which does not agree with Equal Temperament to which your piano is tuned is the fifth harmonic (A, if you are using F as your bass note). When your bass note has been sounded, the fifth harmonic (which gives, in effect, a major third) rings out loud and clear. What, then, if you wish to play the chord of F minor using your bass F as the root of this chord? A♭ is going to clash badly with the fifth harmonic which is A♮. Play the chord of F major, later adding an A♭ softly at the pitch of the fifth harmonic. *Ouch!* So thought the ancient musicians who decided that any minor chord which has to be sustained for any length became painful, and was better changed to a major chord – especially at the end of a piece – so as to avoid the minor third clashing with the fifth harmonic. This effect is otherwise known as the TIERCE DE PICARDIE.

Do all minor chords have to be changed to major chords? No, they just have to be better in tune to sound right, though if you now play alternate major and minor chords on the piano, you will hear a clarity about the major chord and a bit of *ouch!* in the minor. The scoring of the chord is important, of course, and a well-scored chord can sound 'cleaner'. The pitch of any note can also be changed very slightly on the piano by playing each note with a different nuance: loud = sharper; soft = flatter. A dominant seventh chord will sound better when the seventh is played softly.

Although no flute playing has taken place yet – don't worry! A clear understanding of what has gone before and what is to follow is vital to any future intonation practice.

SCALES

No, not the sort you have to practise to acquire a technique, but the division of the octave into notes and intervals. Music making came first: constructing scales came later to meet the needs of music. In the earliest European music, the need to change key often, as we do today, was not required by composers or listeners. Chord changes were simple. Music was based on the intervals in the Chord of Nature, or the natural Harmonic Series, which means that the notes of the scale match the Harmonic Series you have heard. Unfortunately, the distance between each semitone is not the same. The octave is divided into twelve slightly unequal parts. The notes in this scale when played as chords are pleasing to the ear but if any note of this scale is used as the tonic of a *new* scale, the notes in the new key wouldn't correspond with the notes of the old key. In other words, as the music changed into more remote keys, it would sound less and less pleasing.

If one wants to modulate into other keys, the best compromise is to divide the octave into twelve equal parts, the Equal Tempered Scale.

Here is a diagram which shows the difference between an Equal Tempered Scale and Just Scale or a scale according to the harmonic series.

EQUAL TEMPERED SCALE

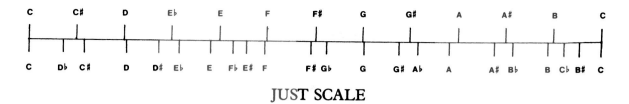

JUST SCALE

Take a ruler and imagine O as C♮, 1 cm as C♯, 2 cms as D, 3 cms as E♭, 4 cms as E♮ etc. The interval C-E, a major third, would appear on the *Just Scale* as about 3¾ cms. Suppose we wanted to use the E (3¾ cms) as the *starting point* to measure another interval. The measurements would not coincide with the remaining measured marks. To change key from C Major to E Major would mean using 3¾ cms as the starting point. To put it another way, imagine a ruler exactly 12 cms long on which the distance between each centimetre varied!

The only sensible solution to our dilemma is to divide the ruler into exactly equal parts, then any point on the ruler can be used as a new starting point.

The same with the octave: divided into twelve equal parts gives Equal Temperament.

The advantages of Equal Temperament are:
1) Changing key, even to remote keys, would sound pleasing on any instrument.
2) All instruments will match each other in scale.

The disadvantage is that: there is a small but discernible 'out of tuneness' in some intervals particularly major and minor thirds.

Look as the diagram again. On the Just Scale there is a difference between F♯ and G♭. Though these are not shown on the diagram, there are also different positions for both double sharps and double flats. To play on a flute constructed to a Just Scale and be able freely to change key, you would need thirty-five notes to one octave and a lot more fingers and arms to play it! As it is, without double sharps and flats, there are twenty notes as compared with twelve notes in the Equal Temperament scale.

In other sections in this book, you will be making experiments to allow you to *hear* these Just Intonation intervals and to appreciate them, though it is not the purpose here to return to the past. Equal Temperament is most certainly here to stay. We have all had our ears trained to hear Equal Temperament as IN TUNE when, in fact, it isn't! One writer referred to it as the Equal T*ampered* Scale.

If everyone were to play exactly in tune with Equal Temperament however, it would sound very pleasing to the ear, or, acceptably out of tune!

When you have fully understood the next section, you will have a clear idea in which direction to move when you are out of tune with another instrument. Playing in tune will follow.

It is a question of a 'good ear' plus ...., ..., and ....!

FLUTE HARMONICS

Now take up your flute and play low C, overblowing it until it plays the octave above. (The same exercise as in Volume 1 – Tone – pp. 6 and 37).

2nd harmonic

The octaves *should* be in tune (but see the section headed THE FLUTE SCALE).

Now overblow C until it produces G.

Quickly compare the pitch with the natural G fingering.

There is a change in quality − ignore this. Listen only to the pitch. There should only be a very slight difference.

Overblow now to the fourth and on to the fifth harmonic − E above the stave. Compare the pitch of the harmonic E with your natural E fingering. You will notice a large difference: the *harmonic* E is considerably flatter and will correspond in pitch with the E♮ in the diagram of the two Temperaments. Continue the series − if you can − to the sixth harmonic − G − and on to the seventh. When comparing this B♭ with the usual fingering, it seems to be neither B♭ nor A, but somewhere in between. It corresponds with A♯ in the diagram on the Just Scale.

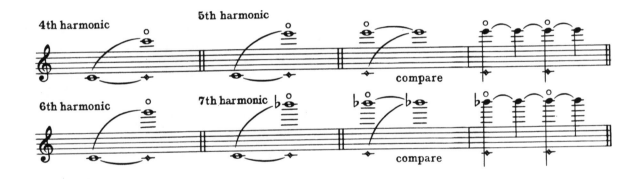

Having observed these differences in pitch between the harmonics and the Equal Tempered tuning on your flute, where does this lead us? Musical scales are made in the process of trying to make music.

It will be obvious that to play in *all* keys at pleasure, the distance between each semitone *must* be the same. This idea of dividing the octave into twelve equal parts is not new, it was first put forward by the Chinese about five thousand years ago and more recently championed by many composers of the eighteenth century including J. S. Bach.

To repeat once more: Equal Temperament means having exactly the same distance between semitones and that, in turn, means division of the octave into twelve equal semitones.

Look at the table below: for simplicity, you will see listed the C Major scale but including an E♭ so that you can compare the C Major and C Minor scales.

A semitone can be divided up into one hundred parts and each part called a cent. There are twelve hundred cents to the octave. In the left hand column are the diatonic intervals from C. Next, are the same notes in cents. The next column contains the intervals in a Just Scale, also divided into cents.

The adjustments which you might wish to make to play *really* in tune are shown in the right hand column headed *Result*. I have measured the amount of sharpness or flatness in pitch required in 'OGGS'. OGGS are anything. I invented them. If you are playing from C to E, then flatten the E by seven oggs, or, quite a bit! The interval C-G is very slightly sharper than in equal temperament.

NOTE	EQUAL TEMPERAMENT (in Cents)	JUST TEMPERAMENT (in Cents)	RESULT THE DIFFERENCE (in Oggs)
C	0	0	0
D	200	204	+2
E♭	300	316	+8
E	400	386	−7
F	500	498	−1
G	700	702	+1
A	900	884	−8
B	1100	1088	−6
C	1200	1200	0

If you really want to sound in tune, you will constantly have to adjust your intonation, depending
(a) on which key your are in, and
(b) on the other instruments playing with you.

I must repeat once again:
THIS BOOK DOES NOT SET OUT TO SUGGEST THAT YOU MUST PLAY ACCORDING TO A JUST TEMPERAMENT SCALE. WHAT YOU LEARN FROM IT IS THAT IF YOU HAVE THE E♮ IN THE CHORD OF C MAJOR IT WILL SOUND *ACCEPTABLE* IF IT IS IN ACCORDANCE WITH EQUAL TEMPERAMENT. IT WILL BE UNACCEPTABLY OUT OF TUNE IF IT IS *SHARPER* THAN EQUAL TEMPERAMENT. IT WILL SOUND PERFECTLY IN TUNE (PROVIDED ALL THE OTHER INSTRUMENTS ARE IN TUNE) IF IT IS FLATTENED BY 7 OGGS *BELOW* EQUAL TEMPERAMENT.

The chart needs now to be translated into intervals in all keys rather than just in C Major and the adjustment you might wish to make committed to memory:

INTERVAL	ADJUSTMENT IN OGGS
MAJOR SECOND	+2
MINOR THIRD	+8
MAJOR THIRD	−7
PERFECT FOURTH	−1
PERFECT FIFTH	+1
MAJOR SIXTH	−8
MAJOR SEVENTH	−6

Notice that if the interval of a perfect fifth has to be made bigger by 1 ogg, the remainder of the octave − a perfect fourth − also has to be reduced by 1 ogg or it wouldn't fit in to an octave! Similarly with a minor third (+ 8 oggs) and a major third (− 7 oggs) to fit into a perfect fifth. The intervals have to be adjusted.

To sum up: read this section again if you are not sure of it. Playing in tune means being able to adjust in the right direction according to the pitch of the other players *or* the surrounding notes. You are not taking a step back into the past. Equal Temperament is here to stay. Clear recognition of Just Temperament enables you to *play* in Equal Temperament *or*, to make slight adjustments according to the circumstances in order to play *better* than Equal Temperament. Put another way, to play *really* in tune.

Finally, the adjustment to the intonation refers to the key you are in. When the piece changes key, the adjustments change, though you will probably not get as far as that stage. It will be found sufficient to *appreciate* the necessary adjustments in the present key.

The following piece is a good example of changing intonation. The changes are *only small*. The asterisks indicate the notes you should be most conscious of. As the piano part is largely arpeggios it is not so important to play each flute note at the same pitch as the piano. If, however, the piano part has block chords – as illustrated for simplicity in the example below – then playing each note at the same pitch as the piano *would* be necessary. You will have to use your judgement as to when it sounds more beautiful to play out of tune with the piano!

MADRIGAL

P. GAUBERT

Reproduced by permission of Enoch et Cie, Paris
UK and Commonwealth agents Edwin Ashdown Ltd.

DIFFERENCE TONES

Now the proof, using your flute. For this next experiment you will need another flute player. The two flutes should be played *without vibrato* or any kind of wobble. Tune the two flutes perfectly to the upper D played forte. Whilst player one is holding his D, player two should play B♭ below it. Immediately an uncomfortable buzz will be heard, the result of interaction between the two notes. This buzz will, on careful listening, be apparent as a very flat B♭ sounding nearly two octaves below. It is a Difference Tone. It is called a Difference Tone because it is a note which sounds as a result of hearing two simultaneous clear tones; it is the mathematical *difference* between the two notes.

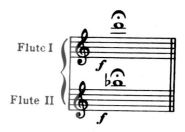

At concert pitch (A = 440 Hz.), the pitch of the two notes is:
D = 1174.6 Hz. (cycles per second)
B♭ = 932.3 Hz.

Subtract one from the other, the difference being 242.3 Hz. which is a little flatter than a B♮ two octaves below. (B♮ is 246.9 Hz.). If you *like* a chord of B♮ + B♭ + D — O.K.! Most people don't, so *reduce* the size of the major third either by sharpening the B♭ or flattening D until the difference tone becomes B♭ exactly two octaves below the B♭ played by the second flute. The chord will then sound in tune.

Notice that raising the lower note or flattening the higher note of any interval *flattens* the Difference Tone.

Now for another three-part chord played by two flutes:
1st flute plays high D again and
2nd flute plays B♮ below it.

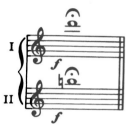

The result is a minor third. But another note way below can be heard. Subtract B from D.

D = 1174.6 Hz.
B = 987.8 Hz.
———————
186.8 Hz.
———————

This gives a difference tone of 186.8 which is very close to F♯ in the low register. What we need to do to make the two notes sound sweet and in tune is to make the F♯ Difference Tone rise to a G♮. To make the difference tone *rise*, the interval has to be made larger. Therefore, the 2nd flute, who plays the B♮, must flatten it with his lips until the Difference Tone — F♯ — rises to G♮, giving a perfect triad of G Major.

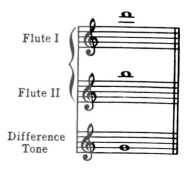

To reinforce this point, all intervals produce **Difference Tones** which can only clearly be heard when the instruments playing them have few, if any, natural harmonics in the tone. Two oboes would be useless for this experiment as they have many natural harmonics sounding with the fundamental.

To further illustrate Difference Tones, here are three trios for two flutes! Careful examination of the chart on page 11 and a careful adjustment of the requisite Oggs will produce the bass line illustrated in the first two trios. Memorise the Oggs chart and use your ears. It is better for one player only to make these adjustments.

ARBEAU-WARLOCK

GOD SAVE THE QUEEN

In this 'trio' the tune appears in the Difference Tones. What is the tune?

Try writing your own trio for two flutes!

Have you been wondering why equal temperament tuning hasn't worried you, or others before you? It has, though music has become so harmonically complex that the differences don't show as much as in earlier, purer music.

Fifty years ago a lecturer on music said 'The human ear is much like the back of a donkey; you can whip it into callousness to almost any kind of harmonic punishment.' How very true that is today.

THE FLUTE SCALE

Before we go further, a close examination should be made of the scale of your flute. During the past fifteen years, manufacturers have gone through a period of re-examination in many aspects of flute making, notably the tone-hole positions or flute scale.

When Boehm designed the modern flute in 1847 he developed a precise method of calculating the position of the tone holes and hence, the intonation.

The pitch in use at this time was A = 435 Hz. or cycles per second. Gradually, between 1847 and 1930 the pitch generally in use rose to A = 440 Hz. Though the flute makers made adjustments to the scale, such as moving the A♮ hole closer to the mouth hole, a rise in pitch would require *all* the tone holes to be moved. Each manufacturer found his own method of doing this and not until fairly recently did any re-examination of the complete scale take place, largely due to the work of Albert Cooper of London. He devised a scale which lowered the traditionally sharp notes in the left hand (C♯ and C♮ etc.) and raised the flat notes at the lower end of the flute. The result is Cooper's Scale, a new scheme for the size and position of the tone holes to enable us to play an Equal Tempered scale without having to make big adjustments with the lips. It is enough to have to do battle with draughty halls, differently pitched pianos, the temperature of the room, and the problems of other players, without having the added problem of one's own flute.

A modern scale flute such as Cooper's will not solve *all* problems. Adjustments will still have to be made in different performing conditions. In general, a traditional scale flute is sharp on some left hand notes and flat in the right hand lower notes, or expressed another way, the octave length of the flute is too long. At the time of this revision, 1991, most manufacturers have adopted the new scale flutes, some completely, and some with their own modifications.

   Check it yourself. First, tune carefully to a tuning fork, then play low C followed by the first harmonic of C. Then slur to the natural left hand fingering of C:

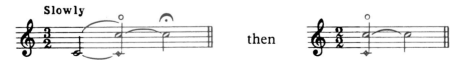

There is a change of tone quality but the notes should be in tune. MAKE NO ATTEMPT TO TUNE THE NOTES WITH YOUR LIPS.

Repeat with C♯:

Do the upper C's and C#'s appear to be sharper than the harmonics? They shouldn't be. If they are, the chances are that your flute is a traditional scale flute. But first, some further checks. If you've already read the section headed THE CHORD OF NATURE you will realise that a perfect fifth is a *near* perfect interval in Equal Temperament. Therefore, also check the fifths:

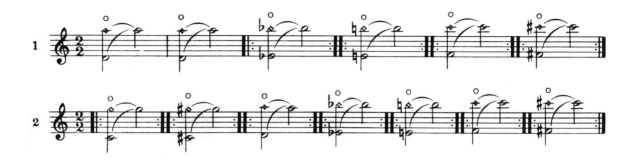

Be sure *not* to move your lips in an attempt to tune the notes. The normal fingering should sound very slightly flat. (1 Ogg!)

Some flutes have, in the left hand fingering a *sharp* C# and a *flat* C♮. These popular flutes also have a short headjoint which complicates things. A temporary remedy is to pull the headjoint out somewhat, though that will make the C♮ flatter still! After careful checking, if your flute seems to need some adjustment you could, if it is a good flute, have the tone holes moved and tuned – a costly business.

Although the right hand notes can't be made sharper, the left hand notes, C#, and C♮, and B♭ *can* be made flatter. With flatter left hand notes, the headjoint can be pushed further in thus raising the pitch of the right hand notes.

Even with a modern scale flute, you may wish to adjust it slightly. Don't stop using your ears, even with a modern scale flute!

POSITIONS OF TONE HOLES CHART

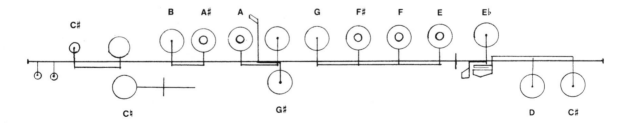

Make a list of notes which you feel are a little sharp. Study the diagram above.
To make some adjustments to your flute you will need some plasticine and a toothpick or sharpened matchstick. Remove left hand mechanism and thumb key (C♮ tone hole). Roll a piece of plasticine between your fingers and thumb and wipe it against the inside edge of the required tone hole as labelled in the diagram, leaving a crescent shaped deposit as shown:

HEAD JOINT ⟵ ◖ ⟶ **FOOT JOINT**

By doing this the vibrating column of air will have further to travel down the tube before escaping and so the note will be flatter. Sculpt the plasticine carefully with a toothpick and remove any from the top of the tone hole so that on replacing the key, the pad will not come into contact with the plasticine. Replace the mechanism. Try the tuning exercise again. If further adjustments are necessary, add or subtract more plasticine.

These adjustments to the tuning will not affect the tone to any discernible degree.
Don't worry about lumps appearing in the bore of the flute. Do not swab out your flute. When satisfied, play it for a week. Then, replace the plasticine (some of which may have fallen out anyway) with a fibre-glass paste or a car body repair paste, widely available. This substance can be scraped or filed away to fine-tune the note. It can also, if required, easily be removed by exerting pressure on it when dried. This technique has a two-fold effect on the scale: it causes the air column to travel farther and it makes the hole smaller, both of which flatten a note.

Some further checks:

It is quite impossible to say what should be done to *your* flute. Each maker has a different scale. Generally speaking, however, traditional scale flutes have a very sharp C♯ and C♮ and a quite sharp A♯ in the left hand. Only F♯ is often sharp in the right hand. From F♮ down, the notes get progressively flatter.

N.B. Be sure the cork in the headjoint is correctly placed. It should be 17.3 mm from the centre of the embouchure hole. Most cleaning sticks have a line engraved at this point which should appear in the *centre* of the embouchure hole. It should *never* be moved from this position as it affects the TONE throughout the entire compass and the intonation of the third octave from D upwards.
The point of this section is, then, to flatten any sharp notes. Flat notes can't be sharpened, but flattening the sharp notes and pushing the head joint further in, will sharpen *all* the notes. If necessary, half of a centimetre could be cut off the socket end of the headjoint to enable the head to be pushed in more, though do take note of the last two paragraphs of the section headed TUNING UP.

PERFECT PITCH

Many players claim to have perfect pitch.

Perfect or absolute pitch is the ability to identify a musical sound accurately without the help of a reference sound. *This ability is rare.* The ability to identify a note by comparison with a remembered note is common and can be acquired with a little effort. This is called relative pitch. Carry a tuning fork around and practise comparing everyday sounds with it. For a few months listen to the tuning fork before going to sleep. After some practice, you will easily recall the pitch of the fork at any time.

TUNING UP

Musical performances are often spoiled by the inability of the young student to tune correctly. Look at these portraits to see if you can recognise yourself:

1 The player and pianist walk on to the platform. The pianist plays an A which is a signal for the flute player to blot out the note he has heard by performing a few short rapid scales or loud random notes. No adjustment to the flute is made. He coughs. He adjusts his music and his tie. After sucking his teeth, he starts to play.

2 This is the timid one; he plays a staccatissimo, pianissimo A, peers down the flute like a telescope, as if he is Vasco da Gama sighting land; nods confidently to the pianist and begins.

3 As above, only this is a more experienced player; he has observed what professional players do at recitals and he imitates their method of warming up. Offstage can be heard the final variation of the 'Carnival of Tunis'; the audience waits expectantly. He walks on; the pianist plays an A, which the flautist disdains; it must be the wrong flavour! He minutely examines a part of the mechanism and nods to the pianist. Very impressive until he begins the first phrase.

The whole object of tuning up is to *tune up*. No player, however advanced, can hope to give a good performance and give pleasure to his audience without first establishing a pitch relationship with the other player or players.

Most often the performer cannot hear the pitch easily and, feeling that he *ought* to be able to, tries to cover his inadequacy. Allow me, please, to let you into a secret: TUNING UP WITH ANY INSTRUMENT, *particularly* THE PIANO, IS NOT EASY. You are not the only one!

Now to practicalities.

How is the tuning best done? Assuming that the section in the front of this book has been carefully read, tuning up becomes easier with a little practice. You must start from the mental position of *not knowing whether you are sharp, flat, or in tune.* Don't try to understand too quickly or you will not understand at all. The problem is to compare, assess and adjust with the pitch of another instrument.

> 'If I don't know I don't know
> I think I know.
> If I don't know I know
> I think I don't know.'
>
> KNOTS – R. D. LAING
> (reprinted by permission Tavistock Publications Ltd)

Try it this way using the upper A:

Make a judgement: are you sharper, flatter, or the same as the two outside notes? If in doubt, guess. Then adjust and repeat. Again, make a judgement. Don't wait. Make an *immediate* judgement, right or wrong. Then, adjust accordingly and repeat. Do this until you are satisfied. *Make certain you are playing with the same sound as when playing your solo.* If, during the piece, you feel that the pitch is still not correct, then re-adjust during some bars' rest or at the end of the movement. A slow, quiet movement may sound slightly flatter than you would wish; before playing slow movements, push the head *in* a little, though do remember to pull the head out again for the last movement. Don't be ashamed or embarrassed about tuning up in public. Take your time.

For the flute, A♮ is not a very satisfactory note to tune to. You will get a better idea of the total tuning by repeating the above with middle D instead of A.
Be in no doubt as to what happens when the head joint is pushed in:
Suppose you tune to C♮ in the left hand, and, sounding flat, you push the head in by 1 cm to sharpen it. The distance from the mouth hole to the C♮ hole is about 27 cm. You have, therefore, shortened the distance to C by 1/27th. The lower C – an octave lower – which has a tube length of about 60 cm has been shortened by 1/60th. As 1/27th is the *greater fraction*, the upper C will have been sharpened by roughly *twice* the amount of the lower C.
When tuning, therefore, it is wise to tune both A and D, lest when pulling out for A, the D becomes too flat.
This underlines the point that a flute can ideally only be constructed to be played at one pitch. One could go further and say that it can only be played at one pitch, by one player at one temperature. Anything else is a compromise. Therefore, D would be a more practical note to tune to after checking A.

VIBRATO

Vibrato is a fluctuation in the flute tone, about three quarters of which is a rise and fall in pitch, the remainder, a rise and fall in volume or loudness.
Read through this section first to see what it entails.
It has been said that vibrato is something a performer should *feel*, not something to be learned. For those who feel it – and produce vibrato naturally – this may be true. For the large majority who can't do it and want to know *how* to do it, it is something that should be studied and correctly learnt. *String players study vibrato in great detail.*
Vibrato has only been in universal use during this century. In the eighteenth century it was used on some long notes as an ornament. During the early part of the nineteenth century, its use increased to marking the high points in a phrase. With the wide acceptance of the Boehm flute, its use increased though each country developed its own vibrato style. In the advent of Impressionism, it was more widely used and has now become part of the normal colouring of flute tone.
If you were to study the vibrato of singers and players you would notice that vibrato rarely goes above seven wobbles and rarely below four wobbles per second. *It is desirable to vary the vibrato according to the mood and the speed of the music, and the octave in which one is playing.*
The exercises which follow will train you in the use of vibrato between 4 and 7 wobbles per second.
There are three basic ways of producing a fluctuation in pitch:
(a) by moving the lips or jaw by alternately compressing and relaxing the lips.
(b) by opening and shutting the throat.
(c) by using the larynx.
(d) by fluctuating the air speed and therefore the air pressure with the diaphragm.

(c) and (d) are jointly the method most commonly used and are recommended because:
 (i) it allows the lips solely to perform the function of forming the embouchure.
 (ii) it allows the throat to remain open and relaxed – probably the most important single factor in tone production.
(iii) it encourages the correct use of the diaphragm for tonal support.
Vibrato is a regular equal rise and fall in the pitch of a note. Rise *and* fall. If the vibrato only rises *above* the note, the ear hears the average or mean pitch which would be sharper. Remember that the flute was once played without vibrato. The production of a clear straight tone is essential before adding any wobble.

STAGE ONE

Play a few long notes without any fluctuation in pitch. Use the abdominal muscles as in sighing. If any involuntary, unwanted vibrato is already being produced, try to eliminate it or see the Problem Box at the end of this section.

When your tone is straight, play a low G holding the flute only with the left hand. Place your right hand on your abdomen and push and relax your right hand alternately rhythmically to achieve an increase and decrease in air speed. Start at about two or three wobbles per second. It is similar to silently saying ha, ha, ha, ha. (See the diagram below.)

When this is working, try to achieve the same result with the abdominal muscles only, holding the flute with both hands. *The movement of the air must be continuous, not a series of jerks.*

The movement in pitch, too, must go above and below the straight note. *Do* not at this stage assist the vibrato in any way with the throat, lips, arms, or shoulders. Keep still. Persevere with this exercise until it can be done with ease. This may take a few days or a few minutes; do not proceed until you can do this easily. Now play the scale of G, pulsing eight times on each note. Choose a tempo which suits you then try after a time to increase to ♩ =90. Don't let the width of the vibrato get narrower in the middle and upper registers.

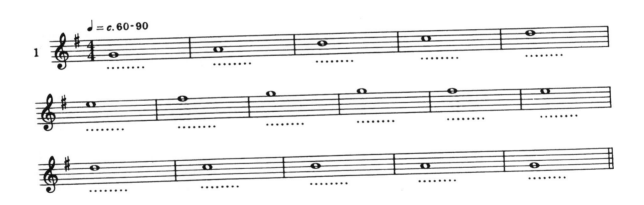

Often the vibrato stops as the note changes. Try to overcome this. Now repeat with six pulses on each note.

Two or three separate ten-minute sessions on these exercises per day will soon produce results. Don't go on until the previous exercise becomes easy.

Time, patience and intelligent work.

Now gradually increase the speed, adding slurs: three wobbles per crotchet.

Be patient: some may find it more difficult than others. Next, find some tunes (hymn-tunes are ideal) in which there are no dotted notes, relatively fast-moving notes, or large leaps i.e.:

Count four pulses (or even six if played very slowly) on each note.
Practise many times each day.
Now for a tune with small leaps. Keep the vibrato moving during the quavers:

Don't stop the vibrato between notes.
Here is another:

PRAISE TO THE HOLIEST IN THE HEIGHT
Adapted from T. HAWEIS, 1734 – 1820, by S. WEBBE

It is a little more difficult to produce the vibrato in the upper register; practise this one carefully. Keep the vibrato going during the quavers:

LET US, WITH A GLADSOME MIND
Melody from Hymn-tunes of the United Brethren, 1824

The minimum time to have spent on the above and previous exercises would be about three weeks; some of you will find a longer time is necessary.

STAGE TWO

Vibrato should not be mechanical and calculated. To progress from Stage One to Stage Two involves trying to allow the vibrato to be a *part of the tone* and not something added to it.

It is a common problem at this point to choose the speed of the notes to suit the speed of the vibrato. In other words you will find your fingers moving after every fourth or sixth wobble even if the piece is slightly unrhythmic as a result.

How to overcome this:

1) Play one of the tunes in this way: play the first note *without counting the pulses of vibrato* and slur on to the next note unpredictably. Some will find this easy, others not. Then play through the tune using much vibrato but changing notes without reference to the pulses of vibrato.

2) Play through your tunes using five pulses to each crotchet, and during the piece, if you happen to use four or six, well, it doesn't matter, does it?

The whole idea of these two ways is to allow the vibrato to be free of the rhythm of the notes so that − like forte and piano − it can become another cosmetic in your musical make-up bag, to be used in the service of music making.

At this stage you may have observed that the abdominal muscles are causing the larynx or throat to pulse in sympathy. This is fine, but *don't assist this throat movement by any sort of tension.* Just let it happen. Little by little the larynx will take over a large part of the work. Any forcing of the throat at this point will result in what was called in the eighteenth century CHEVROTEMENT or a bleating goat vibrato. Save *that* for your old age!

STAGE THREE

(a) Play this exercise. Use vibrato *through* the quavers. Keep the vibrato moving all the time:

(b) Choose other tunes with dotted notes, quavers, etc. but not fast tunes. Be sure the vibrato is ever present particularly on the long notes. For example:

GOD THAT MADEST EARTH AND HEAVEN

Traditional Welsh

You are over the worst; hereafter it's just practice. You, the player, may feel that the vibrato sounds mechanical but your listeners will soon dispel these doubts. This mechanical feeling will soon vanish and vibrato will become part of your tone.

STAGE FOUR

Try to bend *low* C downwards to lower its pitch as much as possible. (See Practice Book Vol 1, page 34). You will be lucky to achieve a true B♮. Now do the same to C an octave higher (left hand C). You may well be able to bend this note down to B♭ or A♮. The blowing tube becomes shorter as you ascend the scale of C and the notes become more sensitive to pitch change. This is important in vibrato practice.

Play the scale of G again:

Without your doing anything to assist it, from G to C the vibrato becomes increasingly wider and, on changing to D, narrower again. It is more difficult to use a wide vibrato when the tube is long.
Therefore, practise slow scales to try to maintain the same *pitch change in the vibrato* throughout the scale.

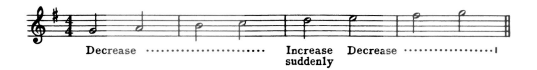

Try other scales as well.
Practise slow scales now throughout the entire compass. The top register may prove to be more difficult and special attention to this register is necessary.

STAGE FIVE

Practise the vibrato at up to and including seven wobbles *per second*. It may begin to even out at six per second until there is an almost straight note. Practice of the earlier exercises, with a wider pitch change will first be necessary. Gradually increase the speed of the wobbles per second.
A metronome is quite indispensable for this.

STAGE SIX

Vibrato should be present but perhaps to a less noticeable degree in moderately moving quavers (say four per second) otherwise the vibrato sticks out as only being used on long notes. Therefore practise this next exercise first very slowly, with a noticeable vibrato, and increase the speed of the rhythm *without stopping the vibrato* until ♩ =c.132.

24

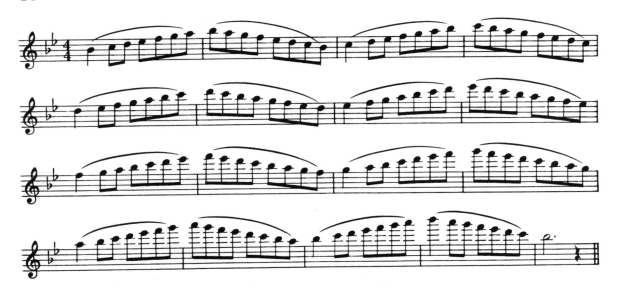

At this point it can *almost* be said that the wobble has disappeared and in its place is a new-found means of expression.

The rest is up to you.

PROBLEMS BOX

1) Vibrato should be *within* and inside the tone, not added on top. If your tone is small, the vibrato should remain within it. Don't transplant the heart of an elephant into a mouse!

2) If your vibrato was achieved naturally and without thinking about it — lucky you. You shouldn't be reading this box because you have no problems! You may however like to join in at any of the stages to *improve* your vibrato.

3) If your vibrato sounds like a goat:

B-aaaaaaaa!

spend a week or two playing long straight notes, at the end of which start Stage One. In all probability, your throat is tense.

4) Watch yourself in a mirror whilst practising. Are your lips moving? Shoulders? Arms? They shouldn't be.

5) A note should start with vibrato. Many pop and folk singers start a note straight, then add vibrato: this makes the performance gimmicky. Avoid it.

FINALLY

When should vibrato be learned? When the tone has been reasonably developed, though it should not be learned simply to paint over obvious flaws. Most young players seem to adjust easily to learning vibrato after two or three years learning the flute, some even sooner.

Experiment with your new-found expression. Slow, low register tunes may sound best with a gently languid vibrato: exciting tunes, especially in the middle and high register may sound better with a faster vibrato.

Occasionally play some eighteenth-century sonata without vibrato. You may well be called upon to do that in an orchestra some day. It is important to be able to play with little or none on occasions. 'The Dance of the Blessed Spirits' (*Orfeo* – Gluck), a pure, ethereal, gentle melody, can sound beautiful in this way. It too often sounds like the hip-swinging dance of a scantily clad chorus girl.

Flute playing is always on the move; changes in style and tone are more obvious examples of changing taste. In the next fifty years one of the changes that must surely come is the control and damping down of vibrato. Its over-use today, especially in eighteenth- and nineteenth-century music, is most apparent in many orchestras where the flutes can often be heard bleating above the throng.

TWENTY FOUR STUDIES FOR INTONATION

Of course, any exercise, played slowly, can become a study for intonation.
These short exercises, one in each key, have used the most common intervals to help you develop a keen 'ear'. They are in order of key but not in order of difficulty; you will decide for yourself which are the most difficult.
Pay particular attention – even with a 'tuned' flute – to the left hand C♯'s and C♮'s, and to the lowest notes.
Most of the exercises should be repeated on octave higher where a different set of problems will arise. *Avoid playing sharp in the top register.*
Practise these studies both piano and forte, and always slowly.

26

A minor

Practise one octave higher

G major

Practise one octave higher

E minor

Practise one octave higher

D major

Practise one octave **higher**

B minor

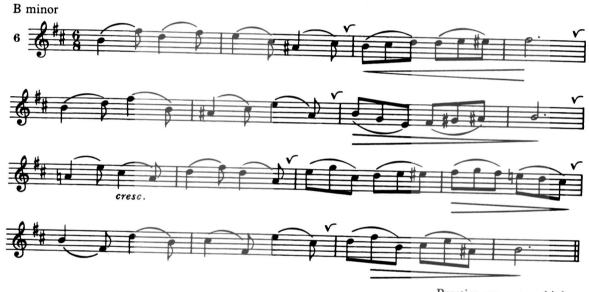

Practise one octave **higher**

A major

F♯ minor

Practise one octave higher

E major

cresc.

Practise one octave higher

C♯ minor

Practise one octave higher

B major

G♯ minor

Practise one octave **higher**

F♯ major

Practise one octave **higher**

E♭ minor

Bb minor

Practise one octave higher

Db major

Practise one octave higher

F minor

Practise one octave higher

Ab major

Practise one octave higher

C minor

19

cresc.

cresc.

Practise one octave higher

Eb major

20

cresc.

cresc.

Practise one octave higher

G minor

21

cresc.

cresc.

Practise one octave higher

B♭ major

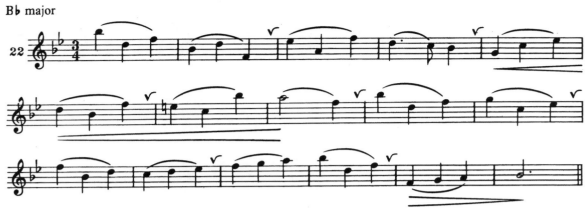

Practise one octave higher

F major

Practise one octave higher

D minor

24

Practise one octave higher

A useful study for intonation is the Tone Colour Exercise in Volume 1 – TONE in this series. It should be practised in all keys.

EXAMPLES OF INTONATION PROBLEMS IN MUSICAL WORKS

For the advanced player, the fingering chart as found in beginner's books is no longer relevant.

There are many special fingerings which resolve some of the problems of intonation. *The 'correct' fingering is the one that is most in tune.*

Here are some examples of possible − or should I say probable! − intonation problems in the orchestral repertoire. Study of these scores in the light of what has been learned will ease many of the difficulties.

I am indebted to Messrs. Roger Rostron and Colin Chambers for assistance in compiling this list.

Top of the list: Mendelssohn *Midsummer Night's Dream Overture.*

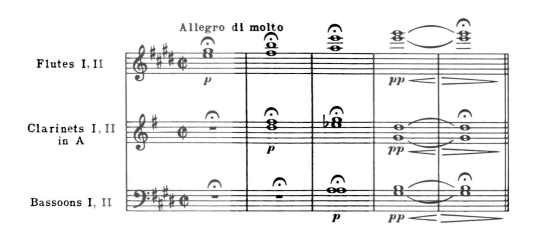

2) Rimsky-Korsakov
   (a) *Sheherazade* − see also bars 314-320, 362-376, 394-401. 1st movement, bar 8 (similar to above). Bars 228 to end in E Major.
   (b) Triplet figure at bar 102 (D).
   (c) 4th movement, bar 655 to the end. The harmonics from 1st desk of violins add problems.

3) Ravel
   Bolero − two piccolo variations.

4) Shostakovich
   (a) *Symphony No. 5* − 1st movement, bar after (39) solo with horn.
   (b) *Symphony No. 10* − 1st movement, two piccolos at end of movement.
   (c) 3rd movement, flute and piccolo in octaves.

5) Tchaikovsky
   (a) *Nutcracker Suite* − 'Dance de Mirlitons' − bar 4: arpeggio.
   (b) *Symphony No. 5* − 4th movement, beginning with bassoons.

6) Verdi
   (a) *Force of Destiny Overture* – bars 51-66, tuning with Oboe and Clarinet.
   (b) *Sicilian Vespers Overture* – bars 14-33, tuning with two clarinets and bass clarinet in E Major.
   (c) *Requiem* – end of 'Lux Aeterna' *pp* to top B♭.

7) Beethoven
   (a) *Leonora No. 3 Overture* – bars 1-5, 278-294, 301-315, 352-360.
   (b) *Symphony No. 7* – 1st movement, bars 56-67 and until 136.
   (c) *Piano Concerto No. 5 (Emperor)* – slow movement.

8) Brahms
   (a) *Symphony No. 1* – 1st movement, bars 1-15.
   (b) 3rd movement, bars 150 to end, but especially bar 162.
   (c) Many of Brahms' Symphonies have movements which end in restrained chords which need careful adjustment.

9) Debussy
   La Mer – 3rd movement, six bars after 54: long solo with oboe.

10) Dvorak
    (a) *Symphony No. 9 (New World)* – 2nd movement figure (1) for six bars.
    (b) 4th movement after the solo, a long diminuendo.

11) Mendelssohn
    Hebrides Overture – last three bars.

12) Mozart
    Piano Concertos – the late ones have prominent wind parts. When the piano has not been tuned to A=440, it can play havoc with the woodwind particularly the clarinets and bassoons which in turn create more problems for the poor flute player.

13) Wagner
    Tannhäuser Overture – bars 82-94 and 184-190: tendency to get sharp with crescendo.

VIRTUS IN ARDUIS: Valour in difficulties!

TREVOR WYE

VIDEO

PLAY THE FLUTE
A beginner's guide

TUTORS

A BEGINNER'S BOOK FOR THE FLUTE
Part 1
Part 2
Piano Accompaniment

FLUTE CLASS
A group teaching book for students and teachers

PRACTICE BOOKS FOR THE FLUTE
VOLUME 1 Tone (plus TONE CASSETTE available separately)
VOLUME 2 Technique
VOLUME 3 Articulation
VOLUME 4 Intonation and Vibrato
VOLUME 5 Breathing and Scales
VOLUME 6 Advanced Practice

A PICCOLO PRACTICE BOOK

PROPER FLUTE PLAYING

SOLO FLUTE

MUSIC FOR SOLO FLUTE

FLUTE & PIANO

A COUPERIN ALBUM
AN ELGAR FLUTE ALBUM
A FAURE FLUTE ALBUM
A RAMEAU ALBUM
A SATIE FLUTE ALBUM
A SCHUMANN FLUTE ALBUM
A VIVALDI ALBUM

A VERY EASY BAROQUE ALBUM, Volume 1
A VERY EASY BAROQUE ALBUM, Volume 2
A VERY EASY CLASSICAL ALBUM
A VERY EASY ROMANTIC ALBUM
A VERY EASY 20TH CENTURY ALBUM

A FIRST LATIN-AMERICAN FLUTE ALBUM
A SECOND LATIN-AMERICAN FLUTE ALBUM

MOZART FLUTE CONCERTO IN G K.313
MOZART FLUTE CONCERTO IN D K.314 AND ANDANTE IN C K.315

SCHUBERT THEME AND VARIATIONS D 935 No. 3

FLUTE ENSEMBLE

THREE BRILLIANT SHOWPIECES

611 (92)

Printed in the EU.